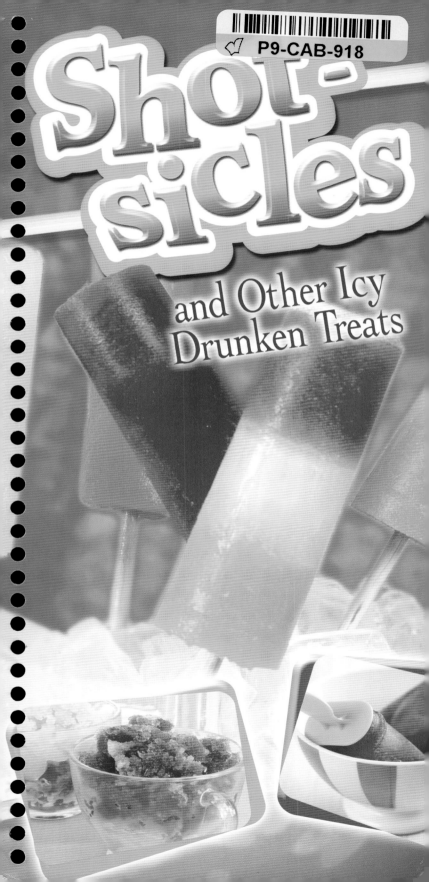

Shot-sicles

and Other Icy Drunken Treats

Recipes in this book are based on the following serving sizes:

Popsicles: 3-ounce molds

Granita-type mixtures: 4 ounces

Smoothies and other iced drinks: 8 ounces

Printed in China

Published By:

 Products

507 Industrial Street
Waverly, IA 50677

ISBN-13: 978-1-56383-399-1
ISBN-10: 1-56383-399-9
Item #7064

Tipsy Tips to Remember

○ A smoothie maker may be used in place of a blender for blended mixtures.

○ When pouring mixture into molds for popsicles, leave about ¼″ headspace (some molds indicate fill lines).

○ When a recipe calls for a carbonated beverage, leave extra headspace for expansion; do not seal, but cover lightly with foil or plastic wrap instead.

○ When freezing creamy mixtures, choose molds without sharp corners for best results.

○ To fill molds easily, combine mixtures in spouted bowls or measuring cups.

○ In place of standard popsicle molds, you can use small paper cups or other small containers and insert sticks when mixture is partially set. Peel off paper cups or remove from containers to serve.

○ Try a variety of sticks with your popsicle molds such as hors d'oeuvre picks, swizzle sticks and wooden popsicle sticks or skewers.

○ If necessary, hold sticks upright in molds by covering with heavy-duty aluminum foil and inserting sticks in the center. Support with tape as needed.

○ To remove popsicles from molds, hold mold between hands or run under warm water for a few seconds.

○ To refreeze popsicles after removing from molds, set them on a platter and return to freezer before serving.

○ To freeze granita-type mixtures, choose a pan (such as a 9″ square pan) that keeps the level of the mixture shallow, allowing it to freeze quickly and evenly.

Rummed-Up Pineapple Sorbet

Ingredients

1 medium fresh pineapple

1 C. sugar

¼ C. lime juice

½ tsp. salt

3 T. **light rum**

Directions

Cut off the leaves and base of the pineapple. Slice off the skin. Quarter the pineapple flesh from top to bottom and cut out the core of each section; discard core. Slice remaining fruit into small pieces and put into a large saucepan. To saucepan, add sugar and 2 cups water. Cook over medium heat for 25 to 30 minutes or until pineapple begins to fall apart and liquid becomes syrupy. Transfer mixture to a blender and add lime juice and salt. Puree for 30 seconds or until smooth. Cool to room temperature and stir in **rum**. Refrigerate at least 2 hours or overnight.

Pour chilled mixture into a shallow pan and freeze until partially set. Scrape with a fork. Return to freezer until firm. Transfer to a blender and process until smooth. Freeze again. Scoop into bowls to serve.

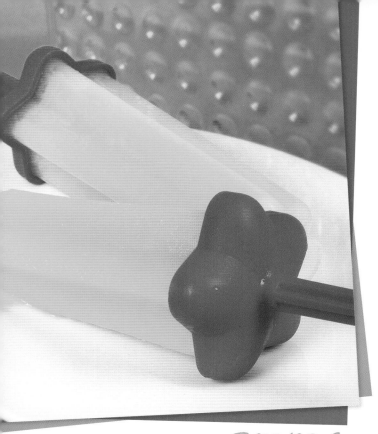

Mango Pops

Ingredients

3 C. peeled and chopped ripe mango
6 T. **light rum**
½ C. sugar
1½ T. lime juice

Directions

In a blender, combine mango, 2 tablespoons water, **rum**, sugar and lime juice. Blend until smooth. Press mixture through a strainer; discard solids. Pour liquid into molds. Freeze at least 24 hours.

Piña Colada Pops

Ingredients

1 (3.4 oz.) pkg. coconut cream instant pudding mix
1½ C. milk
1 T. lime juice
¼ C. **light rum**
1 (8 oz.) can crushed pineapple

Directions

In a blender, combine pudding mix, milk, lime juice and **rum**; blend until smooth. Add pineapple with juice and pulse to incorporate. Pour into molds and freeze overnight or until solid.

Mimosa Ice

Orange Mimosa

Ingredients

1⅔ C. orange juice

2 T. **triple sec**

⅓ C. **Champagne** or sparkling **white wine***

Poinsettia Mimosa

2 C. cranberry juice

⅓ C. **Champagne** or sparkling **white wine***

Directions

For **Orange Mimosa**, in a large measuring cup, mix orange juice, **triple sec** and **Champagne** until blended.

For **Poinsettia Mimosa**, in another measuring cup, mix cranberry juice and **Champagne** until blended.

Pour each mixture into separate shallow pans and freeze until slushy. Stir and refreeze until solid. Scrape surface with a fork and spoon layers of each mixture into chilled serving dishes.

Variations

To make **layered popsicles**, fill molds halfway with Orange Mimosa mixture, tilting the molds and taping to hold in place, if desired. Freeze several hours or until solid. Set molds upright, add sticks and fill with Poinsettia Mimosa mixture. Freeze until solid.

To make a **Lilosa**, use pink grapefruit juice in place of the orange juice.

 * _Try using Moscato or Prosecco._

Serves 6

Irish Nog

Ingredients

4½ C. vanilla ice cream, softened

¾ C. **vodka**

⅔ C. eggnog

¾ C. sweetened condensed milk

2 to 3 T. chocolate syrup

1 tsp. instant coffee granules

1 tsp. vanilla extract

¼ tsp. almond extract

3 C. ice cubes

Additional chocolate syrup and finely
grated chocolate

Directions

In a blender, combine ice cream, **vodka**, eggnog, sweetened condensed milk, chocolate syrup, coffee granules, vanilla and almond extract. Blend until smooth. Add ice cubes and process again until smooth. Place in freezer while preparing serving glasses.

Place a thin layer of additional chocolate syrup and grated chocolate on separate small plates. Dip rim of each glass into chocolate syrup and immediately into grated chocolate to coat. Pour drink mixture into prepared glasses and serve immediately.

Serve-Ahead Tip: Mixture can be poured into a pitcher and frozen overnight. Before serving, stir well with a long spoon and pour into prepared glasses.

Serves 9

Daiquiri Pops

Watermelon Layer

ingredients

3 C. seedless
  watermelon cubes

1 to 2 T. simple syrup*

2 T. **light rum**

Lime Layer

3 T. lime juice

3 T. simple syrup*

1¼ C. lemon–lime soda

¾ C. ice cubes

2 T. **light rum**

Orange Layer

1 (15 oz.) can mandarin
  oranges, drained

1 T. lime juice

2 T. simple syrup*

3 T. lemon–lime soda

2 T. **light rum**

Note: For this recipe, avoid molds with stick/lid combination as sticks will be inserted partway through the freezing process.

Directions

Prepare Simple Syrup as directed below*; let cool.

For **watermelon layer**, place watermelon cubes in a blender and puree until smooth. Measure 1½ cups puree and add simple syrup. Strain mixture into a measuring cup and discard solids. Stir in **rum**. Pour into molds filling them ⅓ full. Do not insert sticks. Freeze 4 hours or until solid.

For **lime layer**, combine lime juice, simple syrup, soda and ice cubes in blender and blend until smooth. Remove any remaining chunks of ice. Stir in **rum**. Pour mixture into molds over frozen watermelon layer, filling to ⅔ full. Freeze 2 hours or until partially set. Insert sticks, pressing the ends just into watermelon layer; freeze until solid, at least 4 hours.

For **orange layer**, in blender, combine mandarin oranges, lime juice, simple syrup and soda. Puree until smooth. Strain mixture into a measuring cup and discard solids. Stir in **rum**. Pour into molds over frozen lime layer. Freeze 8 hours or overnight.

 Simple Syrup: *In a small saucepan over high heat, bring ½ cup water to a boil. Add ½ cup sugar and whisk until dissolved. Mixture should be clear. Cool to room temperature before using.*

Root Beer Pops

Ingredients

3 T. **root beer schnapps**
1 C. root beer
3 T. vanilla ice cream, softened
Additional vanilla ice cream, optional

Directions

Stir together **root beer schnapps**, root beer and softened ice cream. Pour into molds leaving extra headspace and freeze overnight or until solid. If using hollow molds*, use a melon baller to scoop additional ice cream into hollow area. Serve immediately.

We used Prepara brand volcano ice pop molds.

Cosmo-Sicles

Ingredients

- 3 C. cranberry juice
- 1 T. **triple sec**
- 2 T. **vodka**
- 2 T. lime juice
- 6 fresh cranberries, optional

Directions

In a large measuring cup, mix cranberry juice, **triple sec**, **vodka** and lime juice. Place one cranberry in each mold, if desired. Pour mixture into molds and freeze overnight or until solid.

Just Peachy Bellini Pops

ingredients

4 fresh ripe peaches, peeled,
   pitted and chopped

¾ C. sugar

2¼ tsp. lemon juice

1½ C. sparkling **white wine***

Directions

In a medium saucepan over high heat, stir together peaches, sugar and lemon juice. Bring to a boil. Reduce heat to medium and simmer until peaches have broken down and mixture is thick and syrupy, 10 to 15 minutes, stirring frequently. Let cool to room temperature. Transfer mixture to a blender and process until smooth. Add **wine** and blend briefly. Refrigerate until chilled.

Pour mixture into molds and freeze at least 6 hours or overnight. Serve promptly.

 *Try using Prosecco.*

Choco-Sicles

Ingredients

½ C. sugar

3½ oz. bittersweet baking chocolate, chopped

2 T. unsweetened cocoa powder

⅛ tsp. salt

2 T. **bourbon**

Directions

In a large saucepan over medium heat, mix sugar, chocolate, cocoa powder, salt and 2 cups water. Bring to a boil, whisking constantly. Remove from heat; cool 30 minutes. Stir in **bourbon** and pour into molds. Freeze overnight.

"Root Beer" Slush

Ingredients

- ¼ C. **vodka**
- ¼ C. **Galliano**
- ¼ C. half & half
- 2 C. cola
- 6 T. heavy whipping cream

Directions

In a medium bowl, mix **vodka**, **Galliano**, half & half, cola and whipping cream. Freeze overnight. In a blender, process mixture until slushy. Pour into glasses and serve immediately.

Cherry Vodka Granita

ingredients

1 (12 oz.) pkg. frozen sweet cherries

¾ C. sugar

1 T. lemon juice

1 T. **vodka**

¼ tsp. cherry flavoring, or more to taste

Directions

In a medium saucepan over medium heat, bring cherries and 1½ cups water to a boil, mashing occasionally to crush cherries. Reduce heat to low, cover loosely and simmer for 30 minutes or until cherries are soft and juice has reduced by a third.

Meanwhile, in a small saucepan over medium heat, mix sugar and 1½ cups water. Reduce heat and simmer for 30 minutes or until reduced by a third; cool.

Strain cherry mixture into a bowl, discarding solids. Add sugar mixture to cherry juice and stir in lemon juice; pour into a shallow pan. Freeze several hours, scraping mixture occasionally with a fork. Stir in **vodka** and cherry flavoring; refreeze until solid. Scrape with a fork and scoop into bowls. Serve immediately.

Bombsicle Ice

Ingredients

½ C. **blue raspberry vodka**
½ C. light corn syrup
¼ C. frozen lemonade concentrate
4 C. crushed ice

Directions

In a large measuring cup, mix **blue raspberry vodka**, corn syrup and lemonade concentrate. Divide crushed ice among serving dishes and pour an equal amount of vodka mixture over each. Serve immediately.

Choco-Malt Cups

Ingredients

1 C. milk
1 (3.9 oz.) pkg. chocolate instant pudding mix
1½ C. ice cubes
1½ C. chocolate ice cream
¼ C. malt powder
3 T. **chocolate cream liqueur**
2 T. **crème de cacao**

Directions

In a blender, combine milk, pudding mix, ice cubes, ice cream, malt powder, **chocolate liqueur** and **crème de cacao**; blend until smooth. Pour into cups and freeze until solid.

Frozen Mojitos

ingredients

½ C. butter

1½ C. crushed salted pretzels

1 T. plus ⅓ C. sugar, divided

1 (8 oz.) pkg. cream cheese, softened

Zest and juice from 1½ fresh limes

2 T. **light rum**, divided

1½ T. finely chopped fresh mint,
    plus sprigs for garnish

1 C. heavy whipping cream

Directions

Line a muffin pan with paper liners; set aside.

In a medium skillet over medium heat, melt butter. Stir in crushed pretzels and 1 tablespoon sugar; cook for 3 minutes. Remove from heat and cool slightly. Press about 2 tablespoons of the mixture into each paper liner. Freeze 20 to 30 minutes.

Meanwhile, in a medium bowl, beat cream cheese on medium speed until smooth and creamy. On low speed, beat in remaining ⅓ cup sugar, lime zest, lime juice (about ¼ cup), 1 tablespoon **rum** and chopped mint, mixing well.

In a chilled mixing bowl with chilled beaters, beat whipping cream and remaining 1 tablespoon **rum** on high speed until stiff peaks form. Fold whipped cream into cream cheese mixture. Divide evenly among muffin cups, mounding as desired. Cover loosely and freeze overnight or until solid. Garnish with mint sprigs at serving time.

Razzy Yo-Pops

ingredients

2 C. plain low-fat yogurt
½ C. sugar
½ C. frozen raspberries
2 T. **raspberry schnapps**

Directions

In a medium bowl, mix yogurt and sugar.
Place ¾ cup mixture in a blender. Add berries
and **raspberry schnapps**; blend well.
Spoon alternating layers of berry mixture and
plain yogurt mixture into molds. Freeze 4 hours
or until solid.

Tropical Smoothie

ingredients

2 C. lemonade

1 C. lemon yogurt

1½ C. frozen pineapple chunks*

1 C. pineapple sherbet

1 C. ice cubes

3 T. **citrus rum** or **Limoncello**

Directions

In a blender, mix lemonade, yogurt, frozen pineapple chunks, sherbet, ice cubes and **citrus rum**. Blend until smooth. Pour into glasses and serve immediately.

Soak pineapple in **citrus rum** for 30 minutes; drain and freeze.

Serves 30

Red-Hot Grape Pops

ingredients

1 (3 oz.) pkg. grape gelatin

1 (.14 oz.) pkg. unsweetened grape Kool-Aid

1 C. sugar

1 C. **cinnamon schnapps**

Directions

In a medium bowl, mix gelatin, Kool-Aid and 2 cups boiling water until completely dissolved. Add 1¾ cups cold water and **cinnamon schnapps**, stirring until well blended. Pour into molds and freeze overnight or until solid.

Flavor Variations

Cherry: Cherry gelatin, cherry Kool-Aid, sugar, water and **gin**

Lemon-Lime: Lime gelatin, lemon-lime Kool-Aid, sugar, water and **tequila**

Orange: Orange gelatin, orange Kool-Aid, sugar, water and **vodka**

Strawberry: Strawberry gelatin, strawberry Kool-Aid, sugar, water and **light rum**

Punchy Pops

Ingredients

3 C. fruit punch
1 (14 oz.) can sweetened condensed milk
2 T. lemon juice
⅓ C. **gin**

Directions

In a medium bowl, mix punch and sweetened condensed milk until blended. Stir in lemon juice and **gin**. Pour into molds. Freeze at least 4 hours or overnight.

Frosty Sangria

Ingredients

⅔ C. orange juice
⅓ C. **marsala wine**
1 tsp. brown sugar
Cherries or berries, chopped
Ginger ale or lemon-lime soda, chilled

Directions

In a large measuring cup, mix orange juice, **wine** and brown sugar. Place pieces of fruit in each compartment of an ice cube tray. Fill with orange juice mixture. Freeze overnight. Divide cubes between glasses and add ginger ale. Serve promptly.

Lemon-Rum Creamsicles

Ingredients

3 to 4 fresh lemons
1 C. heavy whipping cream
1 C. milk
½ C. sugar
⅛ tsp. salt
2 T. **citrus rum**

Directions

Using a vegetable peeler or sharp knife, remove rind from lemons in long strips. Squeeze juice from lemons to measure ⅔ cup; set aside.

In a medium saucepan over medium heat, combine lemon rind, whipping cream, milk, sugar and salt, stirring occasionally until sugar is dissolved; simmer for 5 minutes. Remove from heat and let stand at room temperature for 20 minutes, stirring occasionally.

Slowly add reserved lemon juice to milk mixture, stirring constantly. Stir in **citrus rum**. Pour through a strainer into a large measuring cup, extracting as much liquid as possible; discard solids. Pour into molds; freeze overnight or until solid. Remove from molds, set on a tray and freeze again for several hours before serving.

Serving Variation

Prepare mixture and pour into a bowl. Freeze overnight. Scoop into dishes and eat with a spoon.

Kiwi Colada

Ingredients

1 (6 oz.) can pineapple juice
1 T. cream of coconut
2 tsp. **coconut rum**
1 to 2 kiwifruit, peeled and sliced

Directions

In a small bowl, mix pineapple juice, cream of coconut and **coconut rum**. Pour into molds, filling halfway. Place two slices of kiwifruit in each mold against opposite sides. Fill with juice mixture and insert sticks between fruit. Freeze 3 hours or until solid.

OJ-Gin Pops

Ingredients

12 to 24 maraschino cherries
1 tsp. unflavored gelatin
4 C. orange juice
½ C. plus 2 T. **gin**

Directions

Drain cherries and pat dry; set aside. Sprinkle gelatin over juice and let stand for 1 to 2 minutes; mix well. Stir in **gin**. Place one or two cherries in each mold; pour juice mixture over cherries. Freeze overnight or until solid.

Grasshopper

Ingredients

2 C. vanilla ice cream

¾ C. whipped topping, thawed

3 T. green **crème de menthe**

2 T. **crème de cacao**

1 T. **triple sec**

1 chocolate cookie, crushed, optional

Directions

In a blender, combine ice cream, whipped topping, **crème de menthe**, **crème de cacao** and **triple sec**. Blend until smooth and thick. Pour into chilled glasses and sprinkle with cookie crumbs, if desired. Serve immediately.

Variation

Grasshopper Pops: In a blender, combine 4½ tablespoons **green crème de menthe**, 3½ tablespoons **crème de cacao**, 3 cups vanilla ice cream, 8 ice cubes and ¼ cup heavy whipping cream. Blend until smooth. Pour into molds and freeze overnight. To cover pops in chocolate, remove from molds; return to freezer for 30 minutes. Melt 1 cup chocolate candy wafers (or chocolate chips with 1 tablespoon shortening), stirring until smooth; let stand until cool but still liquid. Dip top half of pops in melted chocolate and quickly press tip into chocolate cookie crumbs, if desired. Return to freezer until serving time.

White Russian Granita

Ingredients

½ C. sugar

3 to 4 tsp. instant coffee granules

1 T. dark corn syrup

½ C. heavy whipping cream

¼ C. **vodka**

¼ C. **Kahlúa**

Directions

In a medium saucepan over medium heat, mix sugar and 2¼ cups water until dissolved. Increase heat to high and bring to a boil. Remove from heat. Add coffee granules and stir to dissolve. Pour into a medium bowl and whisk in corn syrup, whipping cream, **vodka** and **Kahlúa**. Chill for 2 hours.

Transfer mixture to a shallow pan and freeze 3 hours, stirring occasionally. Cover and freeze overnight.

Thirty minutes before serving, set four cups in the freezer. Scrape the surface of granita with a fork and scoop into frosted cups. Serve immediately.

Variation

Make White Russian in an ice cream maker by decreasing water by ½ cup and preparing as directed above. After refrigerating, transfer mixture to an ice cream maker and process according to manufacturer's directions. Transfer to a bowl, cover and freeze for 2 hours or until firm.

Lime-Pear Sorbet

Ingredients

1 (3 oz.) pkg. lime gelatin

¾ C. lemon–lime soda

¼ C. **light rum**

2 T. lime juice

1 (15.25 oz.) can pears, drained

Directions

In a medium bowl, dissolve gelatin in
1 cup boiling water. Pour into a blender with
soda, **rum**, lime juice and pears; blend
until smooth. Pour mixture into a shallow
pan. Freeze overnight, scraping with a fork
occasionally. Mash and scoop into serving
dishes. Serve promptly.

Brandy Slush

Ingredients

1 C. sugar
¾ C. frozen lemonade concentrate
¾ C. frozen grape juice concentrate
1 C. **blackberry brandy**

Directions

In a large bowl, dissolve sugar in 4½ cups boiling water; cool. Stir in lemonade and grape juice concentrates and **blackberry brandy**. Cover and freeze overnight; stir occasionally. Stir until slushy and spoon into glasses; serve immediately.

Creamsicle Freeze

Ingredients

3 T. butter

½ C. flour

2 T. sugar

¼ C. sweetened flaked coconut

2 T. **coconut rum**

3 C. orange sherbet, softened

2 T. **triple sec**

3 C. vanilla ice cream, softened

2 T. **vanilla vodka**

Directions

In a small skillet over medium heat, melt butter. Stir in flour, sugar and coconut; cook, stirring constantly, for 5 to 10 minutes or until mixture is golden brown and crumbly. Remove from heat. Stir in **coconut rum**; set aside to cool.

In a medium bowl, combine sherbet and **triple sec**. In another medium bowl, combine ice cream and **vanilla vodka**. Freeze sherbet and ice cream mixtures for 30 minutes. Chill small serving dishes.

Quickly spoon some of each frozen mixture into chilled serving dishes, filling to about ½″ from the top, swirling or blending as desired. Sprinkle coconut mixture on top, pressing down slightly. Freeze until serving time.

Variation

Sprinkle about 1 tablespoon coconut mixture in the bottom of a paper cone, followed by ice cream and sherbet, filling to about ½″ from top. Sprinkle more coconut mixture over the top and press firmly. Freeze upright until solid. (To freeze upright, turn a 9 x 13″ disposable foil baking pan upside down and cut eight holes just large enough for the paper cones. Set pan upside down in freezer and set filled cones in the holes.)

43

Bombed Pops

Ingredients

1 (12 oz.) can frozen lemonade
  concentrate, thawed

4 tsp. **Limoncello**

4 tsp. grenadine syrup

3 drops red food coloring

4 tsp. **vodka**

4 tsp. **blue curaçao**

4 drops blue food coloring

Directions

In a large measuring cup, mix lemonade concentrate with 2 cans water. Divide mixture evenly between three smaller bowls, approximately 1½ cups per bowl. To one bowl, stir in **Limoncello**, grenadine and red food coloring. Pour red mixture into bottom third of molds and freeze 3 hours or until solid. Reserve remaining two bowls of lemonade.

To one of the reserved bowls of lemonade, stir in **vodka**. Pour white mixture over frozen red layer in molds, filling ⅔ full. Center a popsicle stick in each mold, fastening to hold sticks upright. Freeze 3 hours or until solid.

To remaining reserved bowl of lemonade, stir in **blue curaçao** and blue food coloring. Pour blue mixture over frozen white layer in molds until filled. Freeze overnight or until solid.

> **Note:** *For this recipe, avoid molds with stick/lid combination as sticks will be inserted partway through the freezing process.*

Blue Orange Sorbet

Ingredients

1½ C. sugar
1 T. grated orange zest
3½ T. lemon juice
1 T. **vodka**
¼ C. **blue curaçao**
1 tsp. orange flavoring
¼ tsp. lemon flavoring

Directions

In a medium saucepan over medium heat, mix sugar and 3 cups water until sugar dissolves. Add orange zest, stirring until mixture comes to a boil. Reduce heat to low and simmer for 5 minutes. Remove from heat, cover and let stand for 10 minutes. Pour mixture through a strainer into a medium bowl; discard solids. Add lemon juice, **vodka**, **blue curaçao**, and orange and lemon flavorings, stirring to combine. Cover and freeze overnight or until solid. Remove from freezer, mash with a fork and freeze again until solid. Transfer to a blender and process until smooth. Spoon into serving dishes and refreeze until serving time.

Serves 4

Grapes on a Cloud

Ingredients

48 red or green seedless grapes
¼ C. plus 2 T. **Galliano**, divided
1 C. heavy whipping cream
2 tsp. sugar, plus extra for rolling grapes

Directions

Soak grapes in ¼ cup **Galliano** for 1 hour,
then freeze 4 hours. Beat whipping cream
and 2 teaspoons sugar until soft peaks form.
Stir in remaining 2 tablespoons **Galliano**;
spoon into dishes. Roll wet frozen grapes
in sugar to coat and set in dishes.
Serve immediately.

Blasted Berries

Ingredients

1 C. apple cider

1½ C. lemonade

1 C. frozen raspberries

1 C. frozen strawberries

2 C. raspberry sherbet

¼ C. **triple sec**

2 T. **light rum**

Directions

In a blender, combine cider, lemonade, raspberries, strawberries, raspberry sherbet, **triple sec** and **rum**. Blend until smooth. Pour into glasses and serve immediately.

Try freezing as ice cubes.

Fro-Yo Cups

Orange-Almond Cups

Ingredients

1 C. orange yogurt

4 tsp. **triple sec**

1 C. plain yogurt

¼ C. sugar

4 tsp. **crème de almond**

Directions

In a small bowl, mix orange yogurt and **triple sec**; set aside. In another small bowl, mix plain yogurt, sugar and **crème de almond**. Spoon alternating layers of both mixtures into small cups, swirling as desired. Freeze overnight or until solid.

Variations

Prepare and swirl together two flavors as desired. Freeze until solid.

Blue Curaçao Cups: Mix 1 cup plain yogurt with ¼ cup sugar and 4 teaspoons **blue curaçao**.

Chocolate Cups: Mix 1 cup plain yogurt, ¼ cup sugar and 4 teaspoons **chocolate cream liqueur**.

Key Lime Cups: Mix 1 cup key lime yogurt with 4 teaspoons plain or **lime vodka**, adding neon green food coloring, if desired.

Lemon Cups: Mix 1 cup lemon yogurt with 4 teaspoons **Limoncello**, adding yellow food coloring, if desired.

Sour Apple Cups: Mix 1 cup plain yogurt, ¼ cup sugar and 4 teaspoons **apple pucker schnapps**, adding green food coloring if desired.

Sweet Tarts
Sweet Tart Baby Pops

ingredients

1 (2 liter) bottle orange soda

1 (.13 oz.) pkg. unsweetened
cherry Kool-Aid

1 (.13 oz.) pkg. unsweetened
grape Kool-Aid

½ C. **vodka**

Sweet Tarts candies, crushed

Directions

In a large bowl, mix orange soda, cherry and grape Kool-Aid and **vodka**. Pour into molds, leaving extra headspace; freeze overnight. Remove from molds and roll edges in crushed Sweet Tarts; return to freezer for 30 minutes or until serving time.

Variations

Sweet Tart Scoops: Pour 2½ cups Sweet Tart Baby Pops mixture into a blender. Add 3 cups orange sherbet and eight ice cubes. Blend until smooth and slushy. Pour mixture into a shallow pan, cover and freeze overnight. Scoop and serve in small dishes. Sprinkle with crushed Sweet Tarts.

Sweet Tart Slushies: Dip rim of each serving glass into corn syrup or water and immediately dip into crushed Sweet Tarts. Prepare and blend Sweet Tart Scoops as directed, but pour the slushy mixture into prepared glasses and serve promptly.

Peppermint Shiver

ingredients

2 C. vanilla ice cream

½ C. crushed ice

2 T. milk

1 T. **vodka**, chilled

3 T. **peppermint schnapps**, chilled

½ tsp. peppermint extract

¾ C. heavy whipping cream

1 T. red decorative sugar

1¾ tsp. **cinnamon schnapps**

Candy canes, whole and/or crushed

Directions

In a blender, combine ice cream, crushed ice, milk, **vodka**, **peppermint schnapps** and peppermint extract. Blend until smooth and thick. Place in freezer while whipping the cream.

In a chilled mixing bowl with chilled beaters, beat whipping cream and red sugar until thick and pink. Beat in **cinnamon schnapps** until soft peaks form.

Spoon alternating layers of ice cream mixture and pink whipped cream into glasses and swirl lightly*. Garnish with whole or crushed candy canes. Serve immediately.

 For a clear swirled effect, ice cream and whipped cream mixtures should be of similar thickness and consistency.

Pucker Pops

Ingredients

2 C. grapefruit juice

¼ jalapeño pepper, cored and seeded

3 T. **gin**

2 T. sugar

1 to 2 tsp. grenadine syrup

Directions

In a medium bowl, mix grapefruit juice, jalapeño pepper, **gin**, sugar and grenadine. Cover and refrigerate for 30 minutes. Pour mixture through a strainer and discard solids. Pour into molds and freeze overnight or until solid.

Bullfrog Freeze

Ingredients

¾ C. frozen limeade concentrate
1½ tsp. **triple sec**
3 T. **vodka**
1½ T. sugar

Directions

In a medium bowl, stir together limeade concentrate, **triple sec**, **vodka**, sugar and 1½ cups water. Pour into molds and freeze overnight or until solid.

Raspberry Pudding Shots

ingredients

1 (3.3 oz.) pkg. white chocolate
    instant pudding mix

¾ C. milk

¼ C. **vanilla vodka**

½ C. **raspberry schnapps**

1 (8 oz.) carton whipped
    topping, thawed

Seedless raspberry jam,
    warmed, optional

Directions

In a large bowl, whisk together pudding mix and milk until blended. Stir in **vanilla vodka** and **raspberry schnapps**. Fold in whipped topping. Pour mixture into 2-ounce plastic cups. If desired, place about ½ teaspoon raspberry jam on top of each serving and swirl gently. Freeze 4 hours or until solid.

Variation

Chocolate Pudding Shots: In a large bowl, whisk together 1 (3.9 ounce) package chocolate instant pudding mix and ¾ cup chocolate milk until well blended. Stir in ½ cup **Irish Cream** and ¼ cup **vodka**. Fold in 1 (8 ounce) carton whipped topping, thawed. Pour mixture into 2-ounce plastic cups. Freeze 4 hours or until solid.

Index